WHAT'S COOKING
low fat

Kathryn Hawkins

This edition published
in 1999 by
Parragon
Queen Street House
4 Queen Street
Bath BA1 1HE

ISBN: 0-75252-935-8 (Paperback)
ISBN:0-75253-225-1 (Hardback)

Printed in Singapore

Produced by Haldane Mason, London

Acknowledgements
Art Director: Ron Samuels
Editorial Director: Sydney Francis
Editorial Consultant: Christopher Fagg
Managing Editor: Jo-Anne Cox
Editor: Lydia Darbyshire
Design: Digital Artworks Partnership Ltd
Photography: Iain Bagwell
Home Economist: Kathryn Hawkins
Nutritional information: Anne Sheasby and Annette Yates

Note
Cup measurements in this book are for American cups.
Tablespoons are assumed to be 15 ml. Unless otherwise stated,
milk is assumed to be full fat, eggs are medium and pepper is freshly
ground black pepper. The calorie counts and fat content
analysis do not include the serving suggestions.

Contents

Introduction   4

Soups & Starters   6

Meat & Poultry   48

Fish & Shellfish   110

Vegetables & Salads   142

Baking & Desserts   194

Index   256

Introduction

No one who has more than a passing interest in their health can be unaware of the problems associated with a diet that contains too much fat. A high level of fat consumption is implicated in obesity – and all that that entails – coronary disease, diabetes and even cancer. The message that we should all cut down on the fat in our diets is reinforced every time we go shopping, and it is almost impossible to walk around a supermarket without being beset on all sides by labels proclaiming low-fat this, reduced-fat that and no-fat the other.

Cutting the amount of fat in our diets is, of course, an effective way to lose weight, simply because it will reduce the number of calories we consume, as well as reducing the likelihood that we will contract a serious disease. However, before we cut fat out of our lives completely, it is important to remember that we all need to include a certain amount of fat in our daily intake of food if our bodies are to function properly. Essential fatty acids are needed to build cell membranes and for other vital bodily functions. Our brain tissue, nerve sheaths and bone marrow need fat, for example, and we all need fat to protect vital organs such as our liver, kidneys and heart.

Nutritionists suggest that we should aim to cut our intake of fat to 27-30 per cent of our total daily calorie intake. If your average diet totals 2000 calories, this will mean eating no more than about 75 g/2¾ oz of fat a day. As a guide, bear in mind that most people consume about 40 per cent of their daily calories in the form of fat. Remember, however, that if you are being treated for any medical condition, you must discuss with your family doctor or practice nurse the changes you propose making in your diet before you begin your new regime.

When you are thinking about reducing your intake of fat, it is important to know that fats can be broadly divided into saturated and unsaturated fat. Saturated fats are those that are solid at room temperature, and they are found mainly in animal products – butter and cheese, high-fat meats (sausages, pâté, streaky bacon), cakes, chocolate, potato crisps, biscuits, coconut and hydrogenated (hardened) vegetable or fish oils. Unsaturated fats are healthier – but they are still fats. Your target should be a reduction to 8 per cent of your daily calories in the form of saturated facts, with the remainder in the form of unsaturated fats. These are usually liquid at room temperature and come from vegetable sources – olive oil, ground nut oil, sunflower oil, safflower oil and corn oil. Remember, though, that oil is only another name for liquid fat. Using oil instead of margarine or butter to fry onions or garlic will do nothing to reduce your overall intake of fat.

INGREDIENTS

One of the simplest and most beneficial changes you can make in your diet is to change from full-fat milk, cream, cheese and yogurt to a low- or reduced-fat equivalent. Semi-skimmed milk, for example, has all the nutritional benefits of whole milk but 10 g/⅓ oz of fat per pint compared with 23 g/¾ oz of fat per pint in whole milk. Use skimmed milk to make custards and sauces and you will not notice the difference in flavour. Low-fat yogurt or fromage frais mixed with chopped chives is a delicious and healthy alternative to butter or sour cream.

Most vegetables are naturally low in fat and can be used to make a meal of meat or fish go further. Recent nutritional research indicates that we should all aim to eat five portions of fresh fruit and vegetables every day because they contain what are known as antioxidant vitamins, including beta carotene (which creates vitamin A in the body) and vitamins C and E. The antioxidant vitamins in vegetables are thought to help prevent a number of degenerative illnesses (including cancer, heart diseases, arthritis and even ageing of the skin) and to protect the body from the harmful effects of pollution and ultraviolet light, which can damage the body's cells. Phytochemicals, which occur naturally in plants, are thought to be instrumental in the fight against cancer.

Steaming is the best way to cook vegetables to preserve their goodness. Boiling can, for example, destroy up to three-quarters of the vitamin C present in green vegetables. If you have to boil, cook the vegetables as quickly as possible and avoid over-cooking, which also destroys the carotene.

If you have time, it is a good idea to make your own stock to use as the basis of casseroles and soups. The ready-made stocks and stock cubes that are available from shops are often high in salt and artificial flavourings. Instead, use fresh herbs and spices in the water in which vegetables have been cooked or in which dried mushrooms have been soaked. Liquids in which meat and fish of various kinds have been cooked should be saved, too. Chill the liquid in the refrigerator and you will easily be able to remove and discard the fat, which will have risen to the top of the container and solidified.

Pastas, noodles, pulses and grains can all be used in the low-fat diet, and they are useful for bulking out dishes. Pasta is available in a wide range of shapes and patterns, and it is an excellent food for boosting your carbohydrate intake. Inadequate intake of carbohydrate can result in fatigue and poor energy levels. Wholemeal (whole wheat) pasta is also particularly high in fibre, which helps to speed the passage of waste material through the digestive system. Stir cooked brown rice into soups and casseroles to thicken them, or mix one part red lentils with three parts lean minced (ground) beef to make a smaller amount of meat go further. Before you buy, check that noodles and pastas have not been enriched with egg. Look out instead for wholemeal (whole wheat) or rice varieties.

EQUIPMENT

Money spent on good quality non-stick pans and cookware will not be wasted. Not only will they directly reduce the amount of fat needed for cooking, but they will save you time because they are easier to clean. Remember to use plastic implements or wooden spoons with non-stick pans so that you do not scratch the surface.

A ridged frying pan makes it possible to cook with the minimum amount of fat or oil, because the fat drips down between the ridges rather than being absorbed by the food. Woks are useful – though not essential – for stir fries. When you are stir frying, use the smallest possible amount of oil. Keep the heat constant and the food moving to ensure quick, even cooking. Use a non-stick wok, which will help you cut down still further on the amount of oil you need.

Use a perforated or slotted spoon to remove food from the frying pan, so that cooking juices are left behind. Absorbent kitchen paper is useful both for draining surface oil and fat from food that has just been cooked, but it can also be used to mop up food that rises to the top of a saucepan during cooking. Use plain, unpatterned paper so that no dye is transferred to the food.

Soups & Starters

Many favourite snacks and starters – especially those that we buy ready-prepared on supermarket shelves and in cans – are surprisingly high in fat. Next time, before you buy, think instead about making some of the appetizing recipes on the following pages – they will get your meal off to a wonderful low-fat start.

Soups are a traditional first course, but, served with crusty bread, they can also be a satisfying meal in their own right. Although it does take a little longer, consider making your own stock by using the liquor left after cooking vegetables and the juices from fish and meat that have been used as the base of casseroles. Use a potato to thicken your soups rather than stirring in the traditional thickener of flour and water – or, worse, flour and fat.

If you want a change from soup, try a few starters such as a light Cheesy Ham and Celery Savoury or Parsleyed Chicken and Ham Pâté served with a refreshing salad and crisp breads or flavour-filled Spinach Cheese Moulds.

Chicken & Asparagus Soup

This light, clear soup has a delicate flavour of asparagus and herbs. Use a good quality stock for best results.

Serves 4

CALORIES PER SERVING: 236 • FAT CONTENT PER SERVING: 2.9 G

INGREDIENTS

225 g/8 oz fresh asparagus
850 ml/1¹/₂ pints/3³/₄ cups fresh
   chicken stock
150 ml/5 fl oz/²/₃ cup dry white wine

1 sprig each fresh parsley, dill
   and tarragon
1 garlic clove
60 g/2 oz/¹/₃ cup vermicelli
   rice noodles

350 g/12 oz lean cooked chicken,
   finely shredded
salt and white pepper
1 small leek, shredded, to garnish

1 Wash the asparagus and trim away the woody ends. Cut each spear into pieces 4 cm/1½ inches long.

2 Pour the stock and wine into a large saucepan and bring to the boil.

3 Wash the herbs and tie them with clean string. Peel the garlic clove and add, with the herbs, to the saucepan together with the asparagus and noodles. Cover and simmer for 5 minutes.

4 Stir in the chicken and plenty of seasoning. Simmer gently for a further 3-4 minutes until heated through.

5 Trim the leek, slice it down the centre and wash under running water to remove any dirt. Shake dry and shred finely.

6 Remove the herbs and garlic from the pan and discard. Ladle the soup into warm bowls, sprinkle with shredded leek and serve at once.

VARIATION

You can use any of your favourite herbs in this recipe, but choose those with a subtle flavour so that they do not overpower the asparagus. Small, tender asparagus spears give the best results and flavour.

COOK'S TIP

Rice noodles contain no fat and are an ideal substitute for egg noodles.

Beef, Water Chestnut & Rice Soup

Strips of tender lean beef are combined with crisp water chestnuts and cooked rice in a tasty beef broth with a tang of orange.

Serves 4

CALORIES PER SERVING: 205 • FAT CONTENT PER SERVING: 4.5 G

INGREDIENTS

350 g/12 oz lean beef (such as rump or sirloin)
1 litre/1³/₄ pints/1 quart fresh beef stock
cinnamon stick, broken
2 star anise
2 tbsp dark soy sauce

2 tbsp dry sherry
3 tbsp tomato purée (paste)
115 g/4 oz can water chestnuts, drained and sliced
175 g/6 oz/3 cups cooked white rice
1 tsp zested orange rind
6 tbsp orange juice

salt and pepper

TO GARNISH:
strips of orange rind
2 tbsp chives, snipped

1 Carefully trim away any fat from the beef. Cut the beef into thin strips and then place into a large saucepan.

2 Pour over the stock and add the cinnamon, star anise, soy sauce, sherry, tomato purée (paste) and water chestnuts. Bring to the boil, skimming away any surface scum with a flat ladle. Cover the pan and simmer gently for about 20 minutes or until the beef is tender.

3 Skim the soup with a flat ladle to remove any scum again. Remove and discard the cinnamon and star anise and blot the surface with absorbent kitchen paper to remove any fat.

4 Stir in the rice, orange rind and juice. Adjust the seasoning if necessary. Heat through for 2–3 minutes before ladling into warm bowls. Serve garnished with strips of orange rind and snipped chives.

VARIATION

Omit the rice for a lighter soup that is an ideal starter for an Oriental meal of many courses. For a more substantial soup that would be a meal in its own right, add diced vegetables such as carrot, (bell) pepper, sweetcorn or courgette (zucchini).

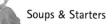

Winter Beef & Vegetable Soup

This comforting broth is perfect for a cold day and is sure to warm you up.

Serves 4

CALORIES PER SERVING: 161 • FAT CONTENT PER SERVING: 3.3 G

INGREDIENTS

60 g/2 oz/⅓ cup pearl barley
1.2 litres/2 pints/5 cups fresh beef
   stock
1 tsp dried mixed herbs
225 g/8 oz lean rump or sirloin beef

1 large carrot, diced
1 leek, shredded
1 medium onion, chopped
2 sticks celery, sliced
salt and pepper

2 tbsp fresh parsley, chopped,
   to garnish
crusty bread, to serve

1 Place the pearl barley in a large saucepan. Pour over the stock and add the mixed herbs. Bring to the boil, cover and simmer for 10 minutes.

2 Meanwhile, trim any fat from the beef and cut the meat into thin strips.

3 Skim away any scum that has risen to the top of the stock with a flat ladle.

4 Add the beef, carrot, leek, onion and celery to the pan.

Bring back to the boil, cover and simmer for about 20 minutes or until the meat and vegetables are just tender.

5 Skim away any remaining scum that has risen to the top of the soup with a flat ladle. Blot the surface with absorbent kitchen paper to remove any fat. Adjust the seasoning according to taste.

6 Ladle the soup into warm bowls and sprinkle with freshly chopped parsley. Serve accompanied with crusty bread.

VARIATION

This soup is just as delicious made with lean lamb or pork fillet. A vegetarian version can be made by omitting the beef and beef stock and using vegetable stock instead. Just before serving, stir in 175 g/ 6 oz fresh bean curd (tofu), drained and diced. An even more substantial soup can be made by adding other root vegetables, such as swede or turnip, instead of, or as well as, the carrot.

Mediterranean-style Fish Soup

Juicy chunks of fish and sumptuous shellfish are cooked in a flavoursome tomato, herb and wine stock. Serve with toasted bread rubbed with garlic.

Serves 4

CALORIES PER SERVING: 270 • FAT CONTENT PER SERVING: 5.3 G

INGREDIENTS

1 tbsp olive oil
1 large onion, chopped
2 garlic cloves, finely chopped
425 ml/15 fl oz/1$\frac{3}{4}$ cups fresh
  fish stock
150 ml/5 fl oz/$\frac{2}{3}$ cup dry white wine
1 bay leaf
1 sprig each fresh thyme, rosemary
  and oregano

450 g/1 lb firm white fish fillets (such
  as cod, monkfish or halibut),
  skinned and cut into 2.5 cm/1 inch
  cubes
450 g/1 lb fresh mussels, prepared
400 g/14 oz can chopped tomatoes
225 g/8 oz peeled prawns (shrimp),
  thawed if frozen

salt and pepper
sprigs of thyme, to garnish

TO SERVE:
lemon wedges
4 slices toasted French bread, rubbed
  with cut garlic clove

1 Heat the oil in a large saucepan and gently fry the onion and garlic for 2–3 minutes until just softened.

2 Pour in the stock and wine and bring to the boil. Tie the bay leaf and herbs together with clean string and add to the saucepan together with the fish and mussels. Stir well, cover and simmer for 5 minutes.

3 Stir in the tomatoes and prawns (shrimp) and continue to cook for a further 3–4 minutes until piping hot and the fish is cooked through.

4 Discard the herbs and any mussels that have not opened. Season to taste, then ladle into warm bowls. Garnish with sprigs of fresh thyme and serve with lemon wedges and toasted bread.

COOK'S TIP

Traditionally, the toasted bread is placed at the bottom of the bowl and the soup spooned over the top. For convenience, look out for prepared, cooked shellfish mixes, which you could use instead of fresh fish. Simply add to the soup with the tomatoes in step 3.